THE SECRET TO A GREAT PREACHING MINISTRY

Other books in this series

The Secret to a
Great Music Ministry

The Secret to a
Great Discipleship Ministry

The Secret to a
Great Evangelism Ministry

The Secret to a
Great Leadership Ministry

The Secret to a Great
Preaching Ministry

STEVEN ELZINGA

The Secret to a Great Preaching Ministry
By Steven Elzinga
Illustrations by Steve Lansingh
Copyright ©2003 by the Bible League

All rights reserved. No portion of this publication may be reproduced by any means without prior permission from the the publisher: Bible League, PO Box 28000, Chicago, IL 60628.

Unless otherwise noted, all Scripture quotations are from the Holy Bible, New International Version, ©1973, 1978, 1984 International Bible Society. Used by permission of Zondervan Bible Publishers. Verses marked NKJV are from the Holy Bible, New King James Version, ©1982. Used by permission of Thomas Nelson, Inc. All rights reserved. Verses marked NLT are from the Holy Bible, New Living Translation, ©1996. Used by permission of Tyndale House Publishers, Inc., Wheaton, IL. All rights reserved.

ISBN 1-882536-61-4

Printed in the United States of America, 2003

ACKNOWLEDGEMENTS

First, I would like to thank my writing partner, Mr. Lansingh. Little did we realize this book about an army would turn out to be such a battle in itself. For months, ideas and storylines were emailed between Chicago and Seattle, often to be discarded and rewritten. I think a stronger book came out of the struggle. Thanks, Steve.

Second, I want to thank Rich DeVos, a friend and mentor who helped me see how ordinary people can do extra-ordinary things if given the right teammates and playground to play in.

Third, I would like to thank my friend and ministry partner in the "revolution," Henry Reyenga. He not only helped me think through many of the ideas in this book but also tried them out in his church.

Fourth, I want to thank my troops at the Bible League. "We belong to each other and each of us needs all the others" (Romans 12:5, NLT). Thanks for your support in the mission.

Last, I want to thank God for giving to humanity the love and hope worth telling others — preaching — about.

CONTENTS

PREFACE	1
CHAPTER 1 — A Tale of Two Preachers	3
CHAPTER 2 — Eleventh Wind	15
CHAPTER 3 — The Five Myths of Preaching	21
CHAPTER 4 — First Day of Class	45
CHAPTER 5 — Three Tasks of Every Christian	59
CHAPTER 6 — 200 Miles	83
POSTSCRIPT	89

"How can they believe in the one of whom they have not heard? And how can they hear without someone preaching to them?"

— Romans 10:14

PREFACE

IF YOU ARE NOT A PASTOR, AND YOU ARE READING this book, good for you — I mean, literally, it will be good for you!

If you are a pastor and are reading this book, chances are some well-meaning member of your church bought it for you in the hope that it would:
    1) encourage you in what you are already doing.
    2) challenge you to do it better.

Regardless of the motivation of your church member, why don't you give it a read? You will never look at preaching the same. When you're finished, give it back to the person and make him or her read it, because it may do even more for that person than for you.

1

A TALE OF TWO PREACHERS

JARED SHIFTED IN HIS SEAT, TRYING TO GET A BETTER view between the heads in front of him. The auditorium was ringing with applause for keynote speaker Arthur J. Hopkins, who was making his way toward the podium, but Jared could barely glimpse the man he'd traveled 400 miles to see.

As the clapping subsided, Hopkins gripped the sides of the podium and began to speak. "George Whitefield had a gift," he said, without preamble. "Some say he found it as a young boy, with the constant influx of visitors and travelers passing through the inn his family owned in Gloucester. He found that he could hold an audience's attention. He could speak. And Whitefield was destined to use that talent to play a major role in what was called the Great Awakening — the Christian revival of the eighteenth century."

Jared turned to his wife and whispered an apology, then crept into the aisle and found a better seat as unobtrusively as he could.

"Benjamin Franklin said about this gifted communicator: 'Every accent, every emphasis, every modulation of voice was so perfectly well-turned and well-placed, that, without being interested in the subject, one could not help being pleased with the discourse; a pleasure of much the same kind with that received from an excellent piece of music.'" Hopkins paused, then added in a conspiratorial whisper, "Of course, Benjamin Franklin got zapped by lightning once, so we might take his exuberance with a grain of salt."

Laughter rippled through the crowd. Now that Jared could see Art well enough, he was surprised to find his mentor's hair had gone completely white and his face was gaunt and sallow. He knew it had been twelve years since graduating from seminary, but the toll of time on his professor's face managed to impress the fact upon him in a new way.

"But the pastors of Whitefield's day were not so impressed. Jealous of his popularity with the people of England, they eventually refused him access to their churches. Nevertheless, this man of God would not be stopped. He took the message of Christ to the people."

Hopkins looked down at his notes. "He wrote on February 17, 1739: 'I went up on a mount and spake to as many people as came to me. They were upwards to 200.' He announced that he would speak again the coming Wednesday. Word spread: 'Whitefield is speaking in the open air.' That Wednesday saw 2,000 people gather to hear the young preacher preach.

"Keep in mind there was no sound system back

then," Hopkins said, tapping on the microphone for effect, "but only the God-given voice of a man on a mission. Four weeks later, on March 25, the crowd that gathered in the open air to listen to the booming voice of George Whitefield — a young man of only twenty-two — was estimated at over 20,000." He paused to let the number sink in. "In the space of a few weeks, Whitefield went from 200 to 20,000 people. That is preaching!"

A few more chuckles erupted from the crowd of ministers and church leaders. Jared watched as Art played deftly to the crowd. Art was certainly not as weary as he looked. For himself, Jared feared, it was the other way around.

"Whitefield describes the response to his sermons in these words: 'Having no righteousness of their own to renounce, they were glad to hear of a Jesus who was a friend of publicans and came not to call the righteous, but sinners to repentance. The first discovery of their being affected was to see the white gutters made by their tears'" — Hopkins traced one finger down his cheek as he spoke — "'which plentifully fell down their black cheeks, as they came out of their coal pits. Hundreds and hundreds of them were soon brought under deep convictions, which, as the event proved, happily ended in a sound and thorough conversion.'"

Hopkins took a sip of water, then continued: "Not only did he draw huge crowds in his homeland of England, but upon his arrival in the recently populated New World of the American colonies, the crowds gathered to hear him there as well. In this New World he

preached to Presbyterians, Congregationalists, Episcopalians, Catholics, Quakers, and Moravians — all who were willing to hear the simple Gospel truth. During his lifetime he preached to hundreds of thousands of people."

Hopkins moved from behind the podium and leaned against it. "Impressive, right?" he asked the crowd pointedly, and received murmurs of affirmation. "How many of you would like to have a ministry like that?" The murmurs were louder this time, and a few people even raised their hands, bringing another wave of laughter.

"And how many of you had heard of him before tonight?" The room grew quiet. A dozen people raised their hands, but there was no laughter this time.

"George Whitefield was a great man of God — a gifted communicator. In his day there was not a better-known man in the English-speaking world. But what became of his legacy? When he died, so did his influence."

Jared smiled. It was one of Art's oldest tricks to pull the rug from under his audience like that.

"Let me ask you another question: How many of you have heard of John Wesley?" Nearly everyone raised a hand. "Of course we have. He birthed a denomination — a denomination that in the 200 years since its inception has expanded into 100 countries around the world, can count 10 million members worldwide, and has founded hospitals, universities, and seminaries.

"So what was the secret of his success?" Hopkins

asked as he returned to his notes. "What did he have that Whitefield never had? To put it in military terms: troops."

He left the word hanging there, and Jared could hear hundreds of pencil tips and ball-points scratching against paper in the silence. Jared frowned. He hadn't expected to take notes and had left his notebook back in his original seat.

"The first troop John joined was a rather strange one — his own family. You see, his father, Samuel, was a brilliant, outspoken, and somewhat eccentric Anglican clergyman. His mother, Susanna, was disciplined, outspoken, and also somewhat eccentric. One day she refused to say 'Amen' to his prayer for the king. She explained that she would not acknowledge William of Orange to be the rightful king — to which Samuel declared: 'If that be the case, you and I must part; for if we have two kings, we must have two beds.'" Hopkins paused for chuckles from the crowd. "Fortunately for John's sake, the king died later that year. The couple reunited, and nine months later, in 1703 — eleven years before Whitefield — John Wesley was born."

Embarrassed or not, Jared knew he had to get back to his pencil and paper. He took the pause as an opportunity to return to his seat, hoping his old professor wouldn't recognize the back of his head.

"John's father taught him the knowledge of the faith. In fact, by age twelve, John knew how to read the New Testament in the original Greek. But it was his mother who modeled the secret of the troop. Susanna was the daughter of a minister who viewed the family as — I quote from her biography by John A. Newton — 'a little gathered Church, where prayer, Bible-reading, catechizing, and detailed personal instruction in the Christian faith provide a framework for the whole shared life of the home.'

"Every week, Susanna, mother of eleven children, would take each one aside for an hour to attend to the issue of spiritual progress. She believed that nurturing the religious lives of children was the most important task a person could undertake, and a responsibility God had entrusted to her. John's hour came on Thursdays."

Jared scribbled as fast as he legibly could manage. He wasn't yet sure where this story of Wesley was going, but he knew he'd tried the Whitefield approach until he was blue in the face, and he was willing to listen to any and every alternative.

Hopkins continued: "The Wesley family troop propelled the young man John to an interest in personal transformation — not only how God saves one's soul but also how one's life can be more and more conformed to the image of Christ. To that end, while in college, he started his own troop called the Holiness Club. This was a small group of students gathering to study the Bible, not just to extract truth from it, but also to come up with practical strategies for how the Bible could be lived out in one's life. One of his fellow club members was none other than George Whitefield." The crowd let out a small murmur of surprise, and Hopkins smiled.

"After the Holiness Club, both George and John

went off on their separate adventures but soon reunited when George introduced John to the excitement of outdoor preaching. But whereas George went from crowd to crowd, John organized the crowds into — you guessed it — troops."

Jared circled and underlined the word "troops" on the top of his sheet. While the military term had first struck him as somewhat impersonal, it was beginning to grow on him. What if he could ask for something and his congregation would simply fall in line? As it was, motivating his church better resembled his attempts to get his kids to sit still in the car.

"The large troops, or meetings, which were typical in size and style with the average church service of today, were called Societies. But you could not attend the large meeting unless you were part of a smaller one. And there were various interlocking small-group options: the Select Society, the Band, the Penitent Band, and the most popular, called the Class Meeting.

"The Class Meeting consisted of ten to twelve people. Following a leader's example, each person told how the Word had impacted his or her life that week. It gave the ordinary person an opportunity to speak — to preach, if you will." Hopkins paused, then repeated the point: "It gave the ordinary person the chance to be a preacher. It also gave one of the twelve an opportunity to try out his or her leadership potential at a new level — the leaders of class meetings."

Jared looked up from his notes for a moment to watch Art, and noticed that he didn't look as haggard as he had ten minutes ago. Either his vision was deceptive back this far, or the captive audience was putting some color into his cheeks.

"In the book *John Wesley's Class Meeting*, which I can't recommend highly enough — it's by D. Michael Henderson for those taking notes — Wesley's system is described like this: 'It took no training or talent to be a class leader; anyone could do it. Being a class leader was in no way related to wealth or education or professional expertise or social standing ... but it did demand faithfulness, honesty, and concern for people. Anyone who demonstrated these qualities as class leader could rise to higher levels of leadership.'

"You see, that was the secret. Everyone had a place to preach. Average people could excel at some troop level. In the 'everyone gets a chance to play' environment, leadership potential was open to all — with the best rising to the new levels of leadership. Those who were gifted were encouraged by the group to advance to the next level. This meant that all members, from the marginally to the magnificently gifted, were encouraged to develop their 'pastor' potential. All had a chance to play the game at their own level. The best — by divine will, blessing, and opportunity — rose to leadership opportunities. All were in the Lord's army, and a person's leadership level was discovered and honed in the trenches of personal relationships: marriage, family, and community."

Jared chewed his pencil's eraser distractedly, searching his mind for a fleeting phrase that had passed through. After a moment, he circled, "Everyone becomes a preacher," on his notepad, then scrawled, "Teach a man to teach others how to fish, and you feed a village forever."

When Jared came back to the lecture, Hopkins was speaking of Wesley's death. "In John 15:16, Jesus says, 'You did not choose me, but I chose you and appointed you to go and bear fruit — fruit that will last.' Although he didn't know it at the time, Wesley's fruit would last, and would influence the world far more than his popular contemporary. Because of Wesley's belief in using the average person, there is a Methodist Church in almost every town in America.

"Here's the question I'll leave you with, folks: Are you working toward tomorrow only, or are you working also toward the next twenty, fifty, hundred years? What spiritual legacy will you leave?"

2

ELEVENTH WIND

"TO STAY OR NOT TO STAY — THAT IS THE QUESTION?" Art asked Jared, his eyebrow raised in a whimsical manner.

"Essentially, yes," Jared answered, chuckling. "You always had a way of clarifying the complex."

Teacher and learner sat in the corner of the dimly lit hotel lobby, cradling paper cups of vending-machine coffee in their hands and trying to keep their voices low. Jared felt guilty about keeping his mentor awake so late, but Art had insisted on an update of his life.

"So, tell me: Did you feel discontent in your job before or after you got this call to start at a new church?"

"Oh, much before," Jared sighed, leaning back in his overstuffed chair. "I've been down and out a lot of times in the past five or six years. I always get a second wind, though — I redouble my efforts, and I'm OK for a while longer. But once I started needing a tenth and eleventh wind, I got the feeling there was something deeper I needed to deal with if I wanted to be really fulfilled in my ministry." He took a swallow of coffee. "But I suppose I never thought seriously of leaving until I got this offer from

Trinity. I didn't even realize how down I was until I got this glimmer of hope that I could start over."

Art nodded. "But you wonder if your problems will just follow you there."

"Right. Maybe it's not my church. Maybe it's me. There was a point at which I felt I was in the top tier of preachers — I had all the tricks of the trade under my belt and could put together a fresh and lively sermon week after week. I think what kept me going those first few years — what kept me working hard, improving my sermon writing and delivery — was largely the satisfaction of a job well done. But after a few years, when I finally looked up from my notes and looked out at the people to see whether they were actually changing or not, I began to have real questions about how well I was doing. I feel like I need to overhaul my approach, but I'm not really sure how, and I'm not sure how my congregation would accept it."

"Hence the impulse to leave. You can dispense with the way it's 'always been done' and start again."

"Exactly. Only — I got a fax from the search committee at Trinity just before I left, and they seem to have a very specific, and very proficient, type of minister in mind." Jared let out a long sigh. "I don't know — I feel like I have to be a Billy Graham just to survive in this arena. I feel like the whole operation hinges on me and whether or not I can hit a homer from the pulpit. A few singles, a few groundouts, and they'll be looking to the bullpen."

"I wasn't aware Billy Graham played baseball," Art said flatly, and it took Jared a second to realize his mentor was teasing him.

"Let me make sure I understand," Art continued, clasping his hands together thoughtfully. "What kinds of expectations did Trinity mention?"

"I don't remember the specific phrases, but it said something like ... ." Jared stared at the floor while he tried to remember. "It was something about delivering sermons that instruct people and inspire them, sermons that convert, nurture, and transform people. I'd like to think that I've accomplished some of that during my decade at the pulpit, but if anyone could do that consistently, then we wouldn't need counselors, teachers, mentors, and artists working at the same thing day in and day out. The thing is, I have these kinds of people in my church, and I think we could accomplish a lot more if I could find a way to harness their abilities to do that type of transformative work. I'm really starting to like your image of the pastor as a general of the troops — to delegate tasks and coordinate the soldiers' movements."

Art nodded. "I'm glad to hear that. I'm glad you're not shrugging your shoulders and resigning yourself to what's typical. I say: Take your time with these questions. Keep seeking and listening and questioning. If you feel trapped between two congregations, consider planting a church where you set new expectations. Or talk to Trinity and share your misgivings, get them out in the open. There is no rule that you can't try something different."

Jared shifted uncomfortably in his seat. "But can I take that risk with so many other people involved? I mean, I have no real plan for how to make the troop idea work. What if it doesn't succeed?"

Art look amused. "It already has, Jared. I've been teaching about Wesley and Whitefield since, well, it must have been just after you graduated. Several of my students have grabbed hold of the army motif and made it work in their churches." He eyes lit up suddenly. "Actually, one graduate — at Cornerstone Church, it's called — ended up only thirty or forty minutes from here. If you have the time, you might visit and see what his church has done with the idea."

"That'd be great," Jared said excitedly, patting his pockets for a pen.

"I'm afraid I don't know the address offhand, but I'll give the pastor a call tomorrow and email it to you." Art glanced down at his watch. "Correction: I'll send you an email later *today*," he said with a groan. "Darlene will have to pack me in the luggage if she's going to get me on that plane in the morning."

Jared apologized and offered a hand to help Art from his seat.

"Give me a call sometime and tell me how your quest goes," Art said as he stood. "I expect to hear great things from you."

"I'll do my best," Jared promised, and shook his friend's hand.

3

THE FIVE MYTHS OF PREACHING

THE HOTEL ALARM CLOCK BEGAN PLAYING STRAINS OF easy listening at ten o'clock sharp. Jared read the time and smiled. It felt nice to be known so well. His wife must have figured out he wouldn't mind missing the first workshop of the day, seeing as he'd tossed and turned until three in the morning, wrestling with new ideas.

Jared had showered, shaved, and half-dressed when he heard the phone ring across the room. Probably Trisha, he thought, calling to tease him about missing out on pancakes at the prayer breakfast.

"Hi, sweetie," he answered.

There was silence on the other end of the line. "No, um, this is, uh, Clive Arbogast. Have I reached Reverend Palmquist?"

"Clive!" Jared corrected, his palms instantly sweating. "I didn't think I'd given you the number here."

"Your babysitter was kind enough to direct me," he said, rolling past the awkward moment. "Listen, I called because the search committee and I are setting down some dates, and it would help if we could get you to commit to an interview next Friday."

"Friday?" He instinctively looked around for his appointment book, then shook his head. "You know, I didn't even bring my calendar on this trip."

"Well, never mind then. It can wait. Just trying to get a jump on things."

"No, I'm glad you called," Jared said. "There are a couple questions I wanted to ask you before we get into the more formal meetings. Hold on." He rushed across the room to grab the coat in which he had stuffed the fax Clive had sent. "It has to do with that job description you sent over," he said when he returned.

"All right."

"There were a few points that seemed, well, like a tall order. Specifically, you say here" — he paused as he unfolded the paper — "that the pastor's role is to 'use the pulpit for communicating, educating, evangelizing, discipling, and transforming the members of the congregation.' Let me ask you: Is this an ideal you're talking about, or an actual yardstick you expect your pastor to live up to?"

Clive thought it over. "Well, we wouldn't expect perfection from a pastor, but it's safe to say those are qualities we're looking for. I don't see what's wrong with finding a person who's a great communicator, a great teacher, and a great leader."

"I see," Jared said, sitting down on the bed.

"Don't you agree?"

Jared sighed. "It might be better to say I have questions. And I'd rather not keep those hidden from you guys if we're going to learn about each other the way we should during this process. Is it safe to assume I can be honest with you and not lose points for it?"

"Sure, I don't see why not."

"OK. I've been struggling with the purpose of preaching these past few years, because to me it seems to accomplish so little. I'm not sure I've found an answer yet, but I know the purpose isn't the things you outlined in your proposal. I've beat my head against those walls too long."

"I'm not sure I understand. They seem like pretty ordinary qualifications."

"Let me take each facet on its own. For starters, you say you want a great communicator. Makes sense. For a long time I believed I was exactly that person. I was so good I could draw tears from a stone." Jared blushed a little at his boast but pressed on. "I had the delivery, the stories, the presence, the vulnerability, and the humor to pull it off with style. But there's something no one ever told me: Speaking through a microphone to a roomful of seated folks is one of the least effective forms of communication. I've read up on this, and researchers have found that, on average, people retain only five percent of what they hear in the lecture format."

Clive jumped in. "But that doesn't make sense. Why would every university in the country rely on the lecture format if it's so ineffective?"

"Well, in a classroom setting you do a lot more than sit and listen to the teacher. You take notes; you read books; you write papers; you study for tests; you do exercises with classmates. There's a whole environment for learning that's created. A church sanctuary is something else entirely — unless you want to prove otherwise by taking a pop quiz on all the sermons at Trinity during the last six months."

There was a chuckle on the other end of the line. "OK, OK — point taken. I'd probably ace the two sermons that I got to preach during this interim period, but I get your point."

"I'm not really saying anything revolutionary. It's common sense that verbal communication is weak — we've let enough words go in one ear and out the other to know it firsthand."

"True enough."

"Now, if we take a closer look at the field of public speaking, I think you'll find that most pastors rate below average compared with others from the secular world. Think about it: How many hundreds of students each year get degrees in communication in order to pursue careers in public speaking, politics, or law? Most of us pastors, on the other hand, got into preaching for reasons other than public speaking."

"Yes, that's true," Clive admitted, "but what you're saying doesn't seem to square with the evidence in that most people in churches across the country love the sermon. Why would they keep showing up if it's so ... forgettable, as you imply?"

"Churches in America are growing at a rate of only one percent each year," Jared countered, "while the population is increasing much faster. We just aren't bringing in many people anymore. Most of the people who love the sermon are people who have been listening to sermons most of their lives. It's a part of their way of life, a part of their community, a part of their past."

"But I got so many compliments on the couple sermons I preached. I'm hardly any good, but people said they loved them."

"That's understandable," Jared said. "Most long-time church people are apt to blame their nodding off on their lack of sleep or their short attention span before they'll blame it on you. They're too full of love and forgiveness to tell you what they really think. If you want an honest opinion, ask an outsider."

"And who would that be?"

"The unchurched. I had a chance to go door-to-door with a friend of mine who was planting an outreach church, trying to listen to the needs of his audience. He asked at every door: 'Why do you think most people don't go to church?' — which, by the way, was a better way to get an honest answer than confronting them with their own lack of attendance." Both men chuckled. "Well, the number-one response he got to his question — which was the same response the twenty other people helping him knock on doors received — which is the same answer thousands of church planters all over North America have been given — was: 'Sermons are boring and irrelevant.'"

"But," Clive jumped in, obviously having readied his retort while listening to Jared's story, "I'm sure they

were just fishing for some excuse to rationalize staying away from church."

"That may be true," Jared allowed, "but only up to a point. Why would so many unchurched people gravitate toward knocking the pastor and his sermon when there are so many other excuses a person could find for not going to church? We might not like to hear it, but there's at least a kernel of truth in their answers."

"I suppose. But that seems to me like an even better reason to request a great communicator for a pastor: to overcome that hurdle."

"All right, let's say you find your man," Jared said. "Let's say Trinity gets a pastor who's in the top ten percent. What does that mean for the other churches out there? Not everybody can be in the top ten percent. What about the other ninety percent who are left with average speakers? I'm trying to think 'big picture' here, and I just don't see how we'll get anywhere if our pastors are slaving away at creative ways to dispense information."

"Well, then what should they be doing?" Clive was sounding frustrated.

"I'm not sure I know yet," Jared confessed. "I don't mean to be argumentative here. I just want to draw you into my dilemma. I have only a wisp of an answer so far: I guess I imagine the pastor to be like a coach talking to his team at halftime. He's not going to give them new information, new plays, or new skills — he's encouraging them, reminding them of long-practiced skills, pushing for better teamwork. The players aren't going to write down an outline of what the coach says — they just need those few buttons pushed to rev them up for the rest of the game."

Jared heard the door handle click open and glanced up to see Trisha enter. She gave him a quizzical look, as if to ask who was on the phone. He held out the fax to her as an answer.

"Are you still there?" he heard Clive ask.

"Still here," he said, looking at his watch as he realized that he might not make the noon workshop either. "I don't suppose I'm keeping you from anything?"

"No, I've got a free schedule. Are you busy?"

Jared laughed. "I should be, but I seem to be on a roll here. I'll be OK if my wife wants to get me something to eat," he said, looking over at her with pleading eyes. She responded with a mock growl.

"Perhaps we can move on to the next issue, then. I suppose you believe that sermons don't educate people, either?"

"Well ... ," Jared hedged, "I want to make it clear that I think sermons can do all these things from time to time. We have all had the experience of learning something new or being transformed by a sermon, and I don't deny that. But I don't see that sermons have a really good batting average. I think there might be more effective ways of doing these things." He paused to write down a shorthand lunch order on hotel stationery.

"If we really want to educate people in the church," he continued, "we can't start in the big group meeting, where we have people of all ages, backgrounds, and degrees of intelligence and knowledge. Educating from the pulpit is like facing the world's worst classroom — you have seven-year-olds who were sent by parents who use church as a babysitting service, fourteen-year-olds who are there because of a crush on a seventeen-year-old in attendance, twenty-year-olds who are on fire for God, thirty-year-olds who have barely heard of Jesus, forty-year-olds who have been going through the motions for years, and sixty-year-olds who probably know more than you do. And on top of that, your class is in session for only thirty minutes a week."

Clive laughed. "That would be grounds for a teacher's strike in any other situation."

Jared missed the rejoinder as he mouthed goodbye to his wife. He plunged straight ahead: "The main problem is: Which people do you gear the education to? There's no way you can meet the educational needs of all, so what demographic do you choose to focus on? In most churches — at least, in my church and some of my friends' — the group that complains the loudest gets the most attention. Now, the kids might wriggle in their seats, but they do not schedule a meeting with you to discuss their frustrations. New people might become bewildered and leave, but they don't have enough stake in the church to tell you what to do. The people who will challenge most pastors about their educational needs are the top twenty percent of Biblically educated people. They have the knowledge-based confidence to challenge any pastor who ignores their needs."

"I've certainly seen that happen."

"So, eighty percent of the congregation falls subject to the trickle-down theory, which is the hope that a highly theological sermon will contain at least one or two nuggets for the less educated to hold onto. But that's not really education."

"Well, what about the churches that are geared toward outreach?" Clive asked.

"It's the same problem, just a different twenty percent being targeted. Then churches have to trust the back-to-the-basics theory, which says that by preaching to newcomers, everyone will benefit from a review of the fundamentals. That's not a bad thing, I suppose, but it still doesn't qualify as education. There's no impetus for growth. There's nowhere to progress to."

"But there are Bible studies and Sunday School and adult education for that sort of thing," Clive countered.

"Yes, precisely. Which is why education doesn't really fall into my job description, at least not in my role from the pulpit."

"OK, checkmate," Clive said with a bit of admiration in his voice. "You seem to know your way around an argument — perhaps I should cross out education and write in 'persuasion' instead."

Jared laughed. "I'm just glad that you haven't hung up on me yet."

"Now, I don't suppose you're going to challenge the sermon's ability to evangelize, are you? I seem to remember something in the Bible about Paul converting thousands with his preaching. Yes, I'm quite sure that's in there someplace ... ."

Jared laughed again. "I won't deny that lots of people have heard the Gospel for the first time and — bam! — they believed. But you can't deny that there are also a lot of people who take a long time coming to a belief in God."

"Agreed."

"Would it surprise you to find out that — in modern-day America, at least — less than one percent of Christians attribute their conversion to an evangelistic service?"

"That can't be right," Clive said. "There are so many people who come forward at altar calls and fill out commitment cards — is that really only one percent?"

"The study I'm thinking of asked Christians what had the most influence in their process of becoming a believer. So, it may be true that many people came to a formal, outward decision when they walked down the aisle or checked a box on a card, but the church service was not what had the biggest effect on them in the whole belief process."

"Then what was the biggest factor in the survey?" Clive asked.

"More than eighty percent said the greatest factor in their conversion was a relative or friend."

"Wow. Eighty percent?"

"More than," Jared confirmed. "And I think it makes sense when you seriously examine what it takes to bring someone from unbelief to belief — at least from a human point of view. I think it takes friendship. It takes walking alongside. It takes people explaining things. It

takes Christians willing to share why they need a Savior, sharing their hurts and pain and struggles. I think it takes people identifying with each other in their hurt. It's an involved kind of thing — much more than a half-hour message is going to offer, no matter how polished or how packed with truth."

"But — sermons are still part of that process, aren't they?"

"Indeed," Jared said quickly. "Everything we say in our sermons can profoundly affect someone's path toward belief. What I'm concerned about is announcing that 'evangelism happens from the pulpit.' The minute you convey that attitude, it lets the average person off the hook. It discourages church members from lengthy commitment to a new person and makes them think that their role in evangelism is inviting a neighbor or a friend or a workmate to church and letting the program take care of the rest. After all, the pastor can talk about Jesus with so much more skill than John Q. Christian."

"So, if I hear what you're saying, you want the congregation to think of evangelism as something they do in their daily lives."

"Exactly," Jared said. "The more we promote evangelism as a kind of quick sell, the scarier it becomes to most Christians, because most Christians are not salespeople. But if I use the pulpit to promote the long-term approach, by recognizing and rewarding people who have stuck with it and had success, I think the church can have a more meaningful evangelism ministry."

"You're talking a lot of sense here," Clive said slowly, as if mulling over his choice of words. "But I have to wonder: If these are such great ideas, why aren't you doing them at your own church? You make a good case, but how does it hold up in the light of reality?"

Jared felt flushed, caught unprepared for an answer. "I have to confess that I don't know. Some of these ideas I've been wrestling with for years; others are brand new in my mind from last night. I feel like I'm getting a sense of how things should be, but I can't quite piece it together yet. I guess I'm taking the time to talk to you now because I want to see if your church is even open to my concerns."

"Well, keep talking," Clive said. "I have to remind you that I'm not the entire committee, but so far I'm listening."

"Right," Jared said, feeling the jitters recede a little. "Then let's move on to discipleship. If you don't mind, give me a definition of discipleship that we might start with."

"I suppose," Clive answered, "that discipling new believers means you're helping them mature in a relationship with God. And to be frank, that's right up the alley of the average sermon, as you're helping people to better understand God and the Bible."

"That's pretty much the standard definition, I'll admit," Jared said. "But I have a problem with it. I can't see how we can judge how well we're doing at it. I mean, at what point can you say someone is now mature?"

"I suppose none of us is ever wholly mature," Clive offered.

"Right, but there must be some goal, at least, that we're shooting for. If we can't know whether or not people are being discipled, who knows if we should rejoice, or fall on our knees in repentance for not being obedient to the Great Commission?"

"Is this a rhetorical question, or do you have an answer?"

Perhaps the Socratic method wasn't suited to Mr. Arbogast, Jared thought. Best to dive straight to the conclusions. "I believe that there's an easy test to measure success in discipleship, and we don't have to look any further than Jesus to find it. It took Jesus three years to make twelve disciples, right?"

"Right."

"He walked with them; He ate with them; He cried with them; He prayed with them; He ministered to them; He challenged them. Then, after He ascended, they went out into the world and did what He had done over the three years. He'd made disciples, and so they did the same. You see, it is so simple: The test of whether you have made a disciple is if your disciple goes out and makes a disciple of his own."

Clive took his time answering. "You're going to have to give me time to wrap my mind around that one, Jared."

"Let me put it another way: To Jesus, making a disciple looked a lot like a mentoring friendship rather than a program or a seminar or a sermon — remember, He spoke to the 5,000, but He discipled only twelve. Day in and day out, He modeled what it meant to live a life

pleasing to God. After three years, His disciples went out and modeled that for others, who modeled it for others, and so forth."

"So, if I hear what you're saying, any shortcut in the process is going to produce a crop of disciples who don't pass anything on?"

"Exactly," Jared said. "If your grandfather taught your father to fish, and he taught you, but you get your son an instructional video, then what is he going to do with his son? I fear that, as the church, we're encouraging our people to use sermons and books and videos as tools for discipleship instead of the blood, sweat, and tears of their own lives. It's a one-on-one, long-term kind of thing. For Jesus, discipling meant spending time with people. That's part of what we need to do to truly follow Him."

"I guess I'd agree with that," Clive said. "But convincing a roomful of reticent churchgoers is a harder task."

"Actually, I see it going on in most churches already, only it's not always called discipleship. When new people walk in the door, and no one reaches out to them beyond a simple hello, they're gone in a few months. But those who get befriended in a deeper way, or join a group where people can care for them, where they can walk through the valleys and climb the mountains together —"

"They stick around."

"Yes. And most often they become leaders, and they create more of these day-in, day-out friendships where they walk alongside someone, crying and struggling and being vulnerable, striving to find out who they are as God's children. That's where discipleship is really happening in our churches, and I think the best I can do from the pulpit is to encourage those efforts. Beyond that, I try to lead by example by making a few disciples of my own — and hopefully start a chain reaction throughout the rest of the church."

"Hmm," Clive said slowly, "I'll have to think more about this method of discipleship. It's not exactly what I'm used to."

"That's all I ask. It's —" Jared stopped as he heard a knock at the door. "Can I put you on speakerphone? That's probably my lunch."

He opened the door, but it wasn't Trisha; it was housekeeping asking if he wanted new towels.

"False alarm, Clive," he said toward the speakerphone as he returned to the other side of the room. He stretched, glad to be out of a seated position at last. "So where were we?"

"I think we were just moving on to the last of our criteria: that the sermons will transform lives.

"Right." Jared began to pace the room leisurely. "This is the most seductive one for me, because I desperately want to believe that I can pull it off. Like a lot of pastors, I went into seminary because I wanted to be used by God. I wanted to see people set free from sin, and to make a difference in the world. So, news of a changed life in my church could fuel my tanks for weeks, even months. It seemed like confirmation that God was using me.

"But somewhere along the line, my self-worth got wrapped up in these reports — more than is healthy. Transformation in people seemed to happen very quickly when I was starting out in my ministry, because I trusted people's compliments that I changed them. But after several years, when I'd preached on parenting for the fourth time and I still saw so many families struggling, I realized that lasting change was a lot harder than a momentary epiphany people might gain from my sermon. My self-worth took a nosedive as I began wondering if I'd had an effect on anyone at all."

"I'm sorry to hear that," Clive said.

"Now, I truly believe that God can work miracles and transform a person overnight. I've seen it happen. But for most people, I think, the transformation takes a lot longer. In fact, I need to look only as far as my own family, and my own parenting, to prove that people do not change easily!" Jared laughed. "I'm still taking one tantrum at a time, still trying to balance discipline and love, still failing and making amends."

"I think we all are," Clive granted.

"So, I decided to investigate some of the stories of change in my church, just to find out what it really took to change a person," Jared said. "I talked to a few people who had started tithing, and found out that one small group had studied the subject and held each other accountable, so they were finally able to break the bonds of materialism. I talked to a couple who had reconciled and found out about their years of ups and downs, the battles and prayer times and tears, the yelling and screaming, the give and take of two people trying to find love again. I asked a person who had become excited about evangelism how it happened — for some reason a neighbor asked her about church, and, in sharing, she went through a process of discovery about what church meant to her. Through these baby steps toward sharing Christ, she found Christ for the first time herself. And through that friendship that developed over the fence, she came to understand what evangelism was and now sees all the possibilities."

"So, you're saying that change happens on God's timing and not ours," Clive mused.

"Precisely. Change happens only by the grace of God, and while it will sometimes be instantaneous, I find that most of the time grace arrives in small measures that get released in the back and forth of a relationship with God, the ups and downs and failing and succeeding. I think our best course of action is to create some room for God's grace to work instead of waiting for the quick fix. There are many concrete things we can do if we ask the tough questions: How many in our church made any significant changes over the last year? What percentage have taken on a new spiritual discipline, overcome an area of sin, or patched up a relationship? How can we make an effort to assist change? What might we do to better assist these types of victories and transformations?"

"And, if I follow your argument, the sermon is not the first place to look for this."

"In my experience, no, it is not," Jared answered. "I deceived myself for many years, thinking that if I could just preach a barn-burning sermon, all of a sudden lives would just transform. The business of changing lives is an inexact and taxing one, I've found, with few signposts and even fewer pats on the back. Yes, my sermons — by the grace of God — have served as turning points or first steps in people's journeys, but in the end they're just one small part of the process."

There was silence on the other end of the line.

"Does that make sense to you?" Jared asked, fearing that maybe he'd crossed the line and come across too brash.

"Yes," Clive answered, "it makes sense. But I'm wondering ..."

The door opened and Trisha walked in, balancing a couple sub sandwiches and large soft drinks.

"Hold on," Jared interrupted, as he unburdened Trisha of the sandwiches. "Hey, Clive, my lunch is here. Do you mind if we continue this conversation another time?"

"Let me ask you one question before you go," Clive said. "What you've been saying makes a lot of sense, and I can see how these requirements could be a burden to you as a preacher — but if you don't believe that preaching does any of this stuff, then what do you believe preaching does?"

This time Clive was left listening to silence. Jared was frozen, his hands leaving the meal half-wrapped.

"If what you're saying is true," Clive continued,

"why should we hire a pastor at all? What is the place of preaching in the church if it's not this?"

Jared felt his appetite disappear. He'd never looked at it from that angle: What was preaching, really? If it couldn't do certain things, what could it do? He looked over at Trisha for help, but she shrugged, having missed most of the conversation.

"Are you still there?"

"I'm here," Jared managed. "I'm still thinking."

Clive chuckled. "Then we've both given each other something to consider. Listen, since you've got to go, how about we both take some time to mull over these issues, and perhaps by the time we schedule an interview we'll have some idea of what our expectations of you should be. Sound fair?"

"Sounds fair," he answered absently. His mind was still elsewhere, frustrated by uncertainty: What *was* preaching, anyway?

4

FIRST DAY OF CLASS

JARED SAT BEHIND THE WHEEL OF HIS RENTAL CAR, staring at the brick exterior of Cornerstone Church. He tapped his fingers absentmindedly against the gear shift. A part of him wasn't sure he wanted to go inside. He'd been glad that Art had set up an appointment for him, but now that he was here his stomach fluttered with nervous energy. The feeling reminded him of waiting in a dentist's office: This might hurt a bit. He regretted asking Trisha to stay at the conference and take notes for him; he could have used her sense of humor right about now.

He was still fifteen minutes early, since he'd left time for misreading his directions, but Jared decided it was best to get it over with. He walked up to the double doors marked "welcome" and gave a pull.

The building seemed empty, so as he walked down the main hallway, he took the opportunity to look around. Walking into what looked like a large, all-purpose room, he felt a wave of nostalgia wash over him. He couldn't quite put his finger on why. Painted on one wall was a large oak tree — or at least the trunk and branches; the hundreds of leaves were made of green paper. He looked more closely and saw that each leaf contained the name of a person and a book of the Bible. Next to the tree was a chart with people's names, and stars marking which books of the Bible each had read. He wasn't sure how large the congregation was, but from the size of this sanctuary he guessed that most everyone was participating.

He continued around the room and saw a wall filled with writing. Painted in various colors were verses from the Bible, each with a date written underneath. He supposed they were part of a Bible-memorization habit of some sort. The next wall featured a few more trees, smaller, and grouped together like an orchard. Each tree listed the name of a church, and underneath the trees it read, "A good tree produces good fruit." He figured these must be daughter churches but was surprised to see so many.

Jared surveyed the room again, and at last he could place that nostalgic feeling. It looked like a grade-school classroom, utilizing stickers, pictures, and progress charts. He chuckled to himself. In a way, it felt like his first day of school, or at least his first day of seminary. On the one hand was excitement about new possibilities and new ideas. On the other was a fear of casting off the old and the comfortable. He was filled with hope that he would discover something truly great, yet he feared that what he discovered would put a blanket of failure over his past.

On his way out of the sanctuary, Jared walked by a table filled with books and brochures, and one of them caught his eye. It had some strange symbols that intrigued him. Jared checked his watch and saw he still had ten minutes until his meeting, so he picked up the pamphlet.

Chapter 4: First Day of Class

SERVING IN THE LORD'S ARMY

"By His stripes we are healed."

> **O**ur struggle is not against flesh and blood, but against the rulers, against the authorities, against the powers of this dark world and against the spiritual forces of evil in the heavenly realms.
> —Ephesians 6:12

Though not found in history books, not portrayed on the news, and not consciously fought by most of the world, there is a battle going on — a war that engulfs all others.

We catch a hint of this war in the sports games we play, the business goals we pursue, the novels we read — all reflections of the one real battle: the battle between good and evil, darkness and light, hope and despair, eternal life and eternal death.

At the formation of the world, a line was drawn in the sand. God created two people and placed them in a garden with two forbidden trees: the tree of life and the tree of the knowledge of good and evil. The battle began when the two people, spurred on by the evil serpent, the Devil, crossed the line.

"So the Lord God said to the serpent, 'Because you have done this, "Cursed are you above all the livestock and all the wild animals! You will crawl on your belly and you will eat dust all the days of your life. And I will put enmity between you and the woman, and between your offspring and hers; he [Jesus] will crush your head, and you [the Devil] will strike his heel." ' " (Gen. 3:14, 15)

You and I are the offspring of the woman. We have been chosen to be God's right arm in battle. Every follower of Christ, without exception, is called to take his or her place on the front lines.

At Cornerstone, we don't want to be in denial about the reality of the battle. Church is not about creating a nice cozy place for fellowship — it is base camp; it is the war room; it is boot camp; it is the troops preparing for D-Day. To that end, we have created a system of military-style ranks to let our members know what their role is in the Cornerstone army, and how they can step up in leadership. This guide explains the responsibilities of each rank.

PRIVATE

Who: Every Christian should become at least a private. No matter how far he or she progresses in rank, the duties of the private are the responsibility of everyone in the Lord's army.

Duties: Every individual is expected to (1) have a daily personal walk with God — listening to God through His Word, talking to God through prayer — and (2) share that walk with others. (Anyone who needs help getting this habit going may ask a friend in the church or visit www.wheresphilip.com for a Bible study focused on personal devotions.)

Purpose: The private level is the basic building block of the whole army. In fact, all the elements of the Christian life are in embryonic form at this level — so every Christian is in training for higher levels of leadership. Not all will make it to the next level, but all should at least die trying.

A WORD ABOUT WALKING WITH GOD:

Every relationship, even with God, is developed through repeated talking and listening.

The most simple and trustworthy way to listen to God is to read the Bible. When you read the Bible, God is talking to you.

Bible reading is not just reading *about* God. It is integral to your relationship *with* God. You need to hear what God has to say in His Word, experience its truth, hear from Him again, experience some more — over and over. Once you have the beginnings of a relationship with God, you start to understand how God talks and the kinds of things He says.

The most basic, simple way to talk to God is to pray. Prayer is talking to a personal God who listens. Talking to God can take on many forms. You might begin with a pattern of praise, confession, thanksgiving, and requests. As you talk more often, you might find yourself praying all the time, without guides to help you.

SERGEANT

Who: A sergeant is the head of a family. Every private in this family is working on a relationship with God, and the group is going to help each succeed. This includes families living together, extended families spread out over distances, and surrogate families for those without blood relatives.

Duties: The sergeant's job is to bring the best out of each member of the family. Every family is expected to meet at least once a week — to talk and listen, sing, read the Bible, pray, and perhaps plan schedules. (Helpful tools for family devotions are available at www.wheresphilip.com.)

Purpose: The family is the heart and soul of the army. It is where bonds are made that last a lifetime. This where the common cause is ingrained. By challenging, encouraging, and honoring the privates in their walks with God, and by keeping them accountable before each other, the sergeant is training each private to one day become a sergeant for his or her own family.

A WORD ABOUT ACCOUNTABILITY:
Our culture teaches us to value privacy and individuality. It can be difficult for us to admit our weaknesses to others. But in an army, the struggle of one soldier is of concern to all. Each depends on the others, and all have a right to know where each one is. The Christian life is not a solo venture.

A WORD ABOUT HONORING YOUR SOLDIERS:
In our world we recognize sports excellence with trophies, educational accomplishment with grades and diplomas, occupational achievements with titles and pay raises. In this church, nothing is more important than that each member have an alive and vital walk with God. We let people know when they are on the right track. Honoring may take the form of verbal thanks, physical awards, or acts of service.

CORPORAL

Who: A corporal is the leader of a small group — a small group of sergeants. A corporal is an experienced leader who, through support and challenge, will train others in how to lead.

Duties: A corporal will run weekly meetings where all the corporal's sergeants will come together. This may resemble a typical small-group gathering, but the corporal's small group is designed specifically to help sergeants succeed in their own mission at home. Weekly meetings offer a time for sergeants to share struggles and encouragement with each other, and for corporals to offer direction and help set goals.

Purpose: Most people are not natural-born sergeants but fell into the role by having kids or being the responsible one in a group. Without a corporal, a family is alone in the battle and may easily fail. But with a corporal, that family has instruction, direction, and support from nearby families — and has a fighting chance.

A WORD ABOUT PROMOTION:

Moving up in rank does not happen for reasons of seniority or even talent. Getting promoted happens only by proving oneself capable at the earlier rank. If a person does not have a daily walk with God at the level of private, he or she cannot be awarded the rank of sergeant or corporal even if the person is leading a family or small group in devotions. A personal walk with God is a prerequisite for being a leader in our church.

A WORD ABOUT HUMILITY:

You will notice that our insignias feature more stripes the higher the rank, but this does not mean that we create hierarchy. Instead, we define a stripe in the sense that Isaiah 53:5 uses it — "By His stripes we are healed" (NKJV). A stripe indicates suffering and servanthood, which our leaders must take on for others. No power belongs to anyone except Jesus, the Head of the army and our one true Commander.

CAPTAIN

Who: A captain will oversee a small number of corporals (small-group leaders) — essentially, be in charge of the health of many groups of families. Captains form the core leadership of the church.

Duties: Captains meet weekly for breakfast with the general (the pastor of the church) and meet weekly with their group of corporals — serving as liaisons between the two. Captains hear about the struggles and successes in each corporal's group and offer recognition, encouragement, and accountability to help the corporals. Captains also convey the pastor's guidance and instruction to the corporals to be passed down the ranks.

Purpose: Captains are the ears with which the general hears about the fitness of his troops, and the mouths through which he directs the troops. This group of leaders allows the army to function as a whole, with all small groups and families working on the same plan instead of each person on an individual spiritual track.

Before Jared could finish reading the pamphlet, he felt a hand tap his shoulder. He turned around to see a tall man with a full mustache dressed head-to-toe in camouflage fatigues. Jared gave a start. Had he wandered into a restricted area of some sort?

"Can I help you?" asked the stone-faced man.

Jared began to stammer something unintelligible.

"Oh, you must be Palmquist!" the man interrupted, his face brightening. "I'm Seth Wagner, the pastor here at Cornerstone." He shook Jared's hand with a strong grip. "I didn't expect you here yet. Let me change out of this costume, and we'll meet in my office."

"Costume?" Jared said.

"Yes, I was practicing a skit with a few others — oh!" Wagner looked vaguely amused. "You thought perhaps we all wore uniforms around here and saluted each other, did you?"

Jared felt himself blush. "No, no ... ," he denied.

"Don't worry — we're not quite that extreme. Listen, why don't you wait in my office down the hall, and when I've changed I can tell you more about how we *do* run things in our church."

5

THREE TASKS OF EVERY CHRISTIAN

DESPITE THE EASE WITH WHICH WAGNER HAD shrugged off any army fanaticism, Jared couldn't help but notice that his office seemed ready for a white-gloved inspection. There were no papers askew, no cluster of photographs, no stacks of books in a corner. The room spoke of discipline — perhaps the only such refuge of order Wagner had in a church filled with construction paper and primary paints.

Wagner walked in, now dressed in a crisp shirt and tie, and grinned broadly. "Glad you could make it," he said, sitting on the edge of his desk and gazing downward at Jared. "Art tells me that you were a student of his almost ten years before I came through seminary — that right?"

"Right," Jared answered, feeling somewhat old and somewhat short in the span of two seconds.

"I owe a lot to Art," Wagner mused. "This church wouldn't exist, you know, if he hadn't gotten me excited with his lectures about troops."

"That's what he said — you'd taken his idea and run with it. I wanted to see for myself."

Wagner did not reply but fixed him with a probing stare. "I see that this is not idle curiosity," he said at last. "You're looking for new ideas, am I right?"

"Right," Jared said again, his voice somewhat shakier.

"Hmm," Wagner breathed. His eyes narrowed. "A lot of people come here looking for ideas, and most of them end up trying out the Bible-reading tree, or the military ranks, or some other piece of the puzzle. I rarely find people who are interested in the key to the whole thing — the puzzle frame that holds all the pieces together."

After several seconds of silence, Jared murmured, "And what is that?"

Wagner just smiled, then turned and sat in his chair at last. "Let me answer your question with another question. What is preaching — in your opinion?"

Jared felt his face flush. "I ... I know a lot of things it's not," he joked lightly, but Wagner didn't smile. "To tell the truth, I'm not sure anymore. I suppose it's a way of connecting people to God."

"No, you're telling me what preaching may or may not accomplish. I want to know what it means to preach to someone. Tell me what it is you do each week putting together a sermon."

"OK." Jared had to think a moment; the process was so ingrained that he rarely considered it. "I pray, and I listen for God to lay something on my heart to say. I read some Bible passages on that topic, and maybe some books. I meditate on it, let it percolate for a while, then write out an outline to speak from. That's about it."

"Simpler."

"Does it get any simpler?" Jared asked with a nervous laugh. He felt like a schoolboy giving the wrong answer. "I pray and listen for a topic, read about it, and then speak to the church."

"You've almost got it now. Boil it down to three words."

"Pray ... read, and speak, I guess."

"Precisely. That's what preaching is all about. You talk to God in prayer, you listen to God through His Word, and then you share that ongoing relationship with other people. Three tasks."

"You make it sound like I'm just doing devotions and talking with a friend about it," Jared said, frowning. "That's simple Christian living, not preaching."

"But simple Christian living *is* preaching!" Wagner boomed. His eyes lit up with enthusiasm. "So much of the world will rub shoulders with God only when people encounter Him in our lives. What you and I do on Sunday morning is a more complicated version of what the individual does, but it's exactly the same task." He clasped his hands together firmly, illustrating his point. "That's the puzzle frame that holds together everything we do at this church: All of us, from me on down to the newest member, are talking and listening to God daily and sharing that relationship with others. We've created a *culture* of preaching."

Jared eyed his fellow pastor skeptically. "I don't want

to sound arrogant when I say this, but doesn't the idea of putting everyone in the church at the same level devalue our position as pastor? What I mean to say is — if everyone can do it personally, why should I preach at all? Why not just let everyone have a turn?"

Wagner didn't answer immediately. Instead he leaned back in his chair and let his gaze drift out the window. A grassy field bordered the church property, and a handful of boys played an impromptu game of baseball on it.

"What game are those kids playing?" Wagner asked absently.

Jared got the feeling he was being toyed with. "Baseball," he answered flatly.

"And what are the rules of baseball?" Wagner turned back to Jared. "Are they any different in the big leagues than they are on the playground?"

Jared contemplated making a joke about the designated-hitter rule but thought better of it. "No."

"So then these kids play the same game as players at the stadium, but they do not take turns with the more experienced players. In fact, they travel to the stadium and watch those games. They go; they get inspired; they learn skills; they have fun."

Jared smiled as the corollary sank in. "You're all playing the same game, then, but at different skill levels," he echoed.

"Correct."

Still, something didn't sit right with Jared. "But that means I have to be playing at the top of my game each week," he said. "What if I go into a slump? That's a lot of pressure."

Wagner smiled. "On the contrary! My church offers less pressure. Think of it this way: If I brought, say, a music fan to the baseball stadium, you'd have to hit a lot of homers in order for him to take much interest. But if I brought a Little Leaguer" — he gestured out the window — "who knows the game and is playing it himself, then he's automatically drawn up in the drama of it. He's there for the love of the sport, not just your entertainment value."

Jared felt himself release a breath he hadn't even known he was holding. He'd never even imagined an audience like that, let alone preached to one.

Wagner was staring out the window again, and seemed to be speaking almost to himself. "I tried to be the star player, too, at first — the kind of shining example you're talking about who's always batting it out of the park. These days I think a pastor should try to help others see that they can be the stars."

"And how do you do that?"

"How do I put it?" Wagner asked no one in particular. He thought for a moment and turned back toward Jared. "When you preach, your goal is not to impress people with what you got out of the Bible, but to impress people with the possibility of what they might get out of the Bible. Your goal is not to have people walking out saying how great their preacher is, but to have people saying, 'I can't wait to do or be something for the Kingdom.' It's about lifting people up, not being lifted up."

The last sentence stung Jared a little; he considered himself a rather humble preacher. Regardless, his face spread into a grin of excitement. Tactful or not, Wagner was on to something.

"So, how do I get what you have?" Jared asked. "I see a sort of chicken-or-the-egg problem on my hands: Do I try to change the people's habits first so that my sermons can be more powerful, or do I change my sermons first in order to inspire new habits?"

It was Wagner's turn to smile. "Good question. I do not want to imply that such changes can happen instantly, or even easily, but there is a definite starting point: Begin with your wife."

"I'm not sure I follow," Jared said, although he was almost certain that had been Wagner's intention.

"I'm going to make the assumption that you have a regular habit of reading the Bible and praying each day. The next step is to talk and listen to God together with your wife. Share what you've been learning on your own. Keep those three parts of preaching in mind: Pray. Read. Speak. Once you've got that going, involve your kids and create a time of family devotions."

Jared stifled a laugh. "You mean that you want me to become a sergeant — to use your metaphor?"

"Indeed." Wagner nodded solemnly. "You might feel you have more important things to do with your time, but let me assure you there is nothing more important."

"Well, I suppose you're right — it's a good idea to have a solid foundation in my life for when ministry gets me down."

Wagner shook his head. "No, no. Your family is not some launching pad from which you do your 'real ministry.' Your family is the key to making a successful church."

"OK, you've lost me," Jared said.

"Let me share a scene from my childhood," Wagner said, his voice slowing into a storytelling rhythm. "Every New Year's Eve, Mom and Dad and my two sisters and I would gather around the dinner table and make a family resolution. One year it was a promise to take turns doing the dishes. We failed at first, like we did every year, because words and good intentions are not enough. But toward the end of the year, Dad began making good on his commitment. I could see how much Mom appreciated that, and how proud she was of him. So I joined in, too. Partly, I think, I wanted to be like my dad, and partly I wanted to do what was right."

Jared nodded. "In other words, 'Do what I say, not what I do,' just doesn't cut it."

"Never did, never will," Wagner said. "A pastor is much like a father to his congregation. While a visiting pastor can sweep in and impress the crowd with some razzle-dazzle, the regular pastor has his whole life open before the people — the good, the bad, and the ugly. The people will be able to tell if the pastor has a walk with God. They see what kind of relationship he has with his wife. They watch his interaction with his children. His people will listen to him based on those criteria, not on how well he can put words together. As with an army general, the right to be heard comes from serving in the trenches."

Jared swallowed hard. "I think I'm starting to catch on. What you're suggesting doesn't sound easy ... but it sounds right."

Wagner nodded.

"So, what's the next step? How do I move from doing devotions with my family to having a whole church on the same devotional track?"

"One step at a time," Wagner said, smiling. "Start by helping other families do the same thing in their homes. Then gather them together for mutual encouragement. Sing songs and share what you've been learning in the Bible; it will even help your habits within the family because you'll all know that you have to perform in the larger group.

"Once you've gathered more families than you can handle, split into smaller groups. Keep meeting with the leaders of the other groups to make sure you encourage and support each other. As more and more people join, deciding to hop aboard the devotional track, your job will get more and more complex. But remember that at each level of leadership your three tasks remain the same: pray, read, and speak."

"What do you mean by getting more complex?" Jared asked.

Wagner thought for a moment. "Let's take the problem of incentive. You're going to find out fairly quickly that people have a deep resistance to doing any sort of 'homework.' With my kids, it was fairly easy to motivate them by offering them a hundred dollars to read the Bible in one year. But that strategy wasn't going to work with my whole church — well, it might have, but I wasn't willing to pay the price!" He smiled. "We ended up finding a cheaper solution: leaves on a tree. It might not be as strong an incentive, but it works well with an entire church because you have enough people to really see the progress being made. It's a bit more complicated to organize, but it's the same hurdle we're clearing."

Jared jumped in excitedly. "And I bet it's a big help to experiment and fail on the small scale before you have a whole church to worry about."

"Indeed. You catch on quickly."

"Oh!" Another connection had made itself clear to Jared. "And that's why you worry when people take only the idea of the Bible-reading tree. It's leaders who are trained to adapt and experiment that makes it work, not necessarily the incentive itself."

"Yes, that's part of it," Wagner said. "Another reason is that any congregation is going to have big objections to signing on to an identical reading track — it doesn't leave room for personal choice; it demands too much time to get through. Most churches aren't equipped to deal with these obstacles, but we were able to overcome them because we have all these various levels of reinforcement. I started preaching my sermons out of chapters in the Bible that were in the reading for the week, and I got my core leadership to follow the same path in their small-group studies, and before long people started following along. They felt left out of the conversations when all their friends were talking about the week's reading, when they saw other people putting leaves on the tree, when they found out I expected them to be familiar with the text when I preached. After about six months, once they realized that this wasn't a passing fad but something I was fully committed to, most everyone began following the reading track. It's really the levels of reinforcement that make our church work, not the visible incentives we come up with."

Jared smiled sheepishly. "Then I suppose I shouldn't ask you about the other incentives I saw in your sanctuary."

"Not at all! They're all concrete approaches to listening, talking, and sharing, so they paint a good picture of what we're about. Ask away."

"OK — I noticed a bunch of verses painted on one of the walls. Were those memory verses?"

"Good observation," Wagner answered. "We have a goal of memorizing 52 verses every year, and then we paint the wall over and start again. Traditionally, we have chosen something out of the week's readings that we haven't memorized in past years. For next year we have talked about memorizing the entirety of a longer passage, along with our daughter churches, and then gathering everyone in the high school stadium for a big singing and reciting event. Again, this sort of memorizing would be arduous for the individual, but corporately we are able to practice together — on Sundays, around dinner tables, in Bible studies. People make flashcards and record tapes for their cars; it's quite an enjoyable challenge."

Jared shook his head in disbelief. "Where do they

find the time to do all that?"

Wagner chuckled. "That's just the tip of the iceberg, Palmquist! Those are just our incentives to help people with listening to God each day. We also want them to talk to God! For that we have a bulletin board where people post prayer requests; we have people get up during the service and share what they've been praying for; we have prayer guides based on the structure of the Lord's Prayer that we encourage people to follow in their daily time with God.

"And don't forget," Wagner said, tapping the side of his head, "that we want people to share their walk with other people, too. Some of that sharing is going to take place within the church, as people share with their families or with the Sunday congregation. But we also encourage sharing with friends and coworkers and family outside the church — not with a goal of selling the Gospel, but simply to share a verse, a song, or a lesson learned that week. For every new person we share with, we write that person's name on a piece of construction paper and add it to the chain that snakes across the ceiling."

"The ceiling!" Jared laughed — he hadn't thought to look there. "And I suppose it's pretty much covered by now?"

"Several times over, actually. I hate to take down a chain, because often people will join our church and we're able to show them their name up there. I love that, because it gives them a feeling of belonging here, a sense of a greater plan for them. Often they can find their name on the chain several times, because several people took the opportunity to share something about God with them. It's a visual history of where God was present in the life of this new person. But, alas, people keep sharing and the chain gets longer. You've heard of people who 'live, breathe, and eat' sports, or whatever their hobby happens to be — they just can't stop talking about it, or using those metaphors, or relating everything to it? That's us."

Jared's eyes narrowed. "So are you saying that everyone is involved in outreach? You don't have a separate Outreach Committee or anything?"

Wagner laughed. "Oh, we've found little use for committees of any sort! I truly believe that the Christian life should not be chopped up into little pieces and divided among labor like in a factory. It's the job of every Christian to do outreach, to practice hospitality, to give to the poor, to disciple other Christians, to praise God in song, and so on and so forth. Putting a committee in charge of something tells people that they don't have to worry about it anymore. Getting everyone involved, and letting a few key mentors rise to the top based on God's blessings of talent and opportunities — that's the way to go."

Jared started to say something, then stopped and frowned. "I don't know if I'd like that. I find that when I delegate things to committees, they get better input than I get all on my own."

"Then I'll put it another way: We're a church full of committees — every family, every Bible study, every group of leaders is a small committee that discusses most every issue we face as a church. When the time comes to make a decision, I can ask my captains for the thoughts and feelings of everyone under them and can weigh their opinions accordingly. That way, everyone has a voice — not just the loud people or the brainiest people or those who live next door to a committee member."

"OK, I see that," Jared said hurriedly, "but the decisions still come down to you, right? Doesn't that make you something of, well, a dictator?"

Wagner was silent. He stared at the floor for a moment, then turned his gaze outside. Jared's palms began to sweat, and he was about to apologize when Wagner said, "It's a nice day out. Why don't we go for a walk?"

The two pastors walked along the sidewalk outside Cornerstone's building. On the other side of the road was the park where the kids were playing baseball, but for some reason Wagner was more interested in walking on the side with office buildings, traffic congestion, and construction projects.

"I will admit," Wagner said at last, "that I have been known to carry this army motif too far. My people joke that I'm going to toss so-and-so into the brig, or hold white-gloved inspections of the resource room. And I'm ashamed to say that's not too far from the truth — I can go right off the deep end sometimes. Whenever that happens I repent and feel terrible, and I offer to just ditch this military thing. But my people never let me. That always brings me back to earth: to be reminded there's a whole team at work and this church is bigger than just me."

He smiled. Jared could breathe again.

"To be frank," Wagner continued, "I'd be even more tempted to believe in the applause and think that I know better if I didn't have this military structure. A good general is responsive to the concerns of the lower ranks, because those are the people on the front lines. I have a network of people designed to tell me what our needs are, and a leadership team to make plans that address them. As a general, I don't just come up with stuff and pass it down the line — I respond to the real battles we're facing as a church."

Jared nimbly dodged a teenager skateboarding down the sidewalk. "I can see that," he said. "But don't these levels still create a pecking order within the church?"

Wagner stopped and smiled. "What group doesn't have a pecking order?" he asked, his head swiveling. "Just look around us."

Jared looked around tentatively, and realized why Wagner had chosen this route. Jared had, quite literally, walked into Wagner's trap.

"The organizational structure of the army is no different than that of any organization," Wagner said, almost giddy. He pointed to a few orange-shirted men filling potholes. "What ranks do you see there?"

"A few workers," Jared said without enthusiasm. "And probably a foreman of some sort."

"Don't forget the invisible parties, like project leaders and owners. Let's try another one: What ranks do you see over there?" A school bus was attempting to merge out of a blocked lane.

Chapter 5: Three Tasks of Every Christian **75**

"Well, counting the invisible people," Jared said slowly, hoping to locate a flaw in Wagner's example, "I suppose there are students, teachers, and a principal. And a superintendent."

"Good. Now try over there." Wagner was pointing to a young mother pushing a stroller and pulling a five-year-old in tow.

"A family?"

"Indeed," Wagner said, still smiling. "Every person in a family starts out as a child — a private, if you will. When you get married and have children, you get promoted to sergeant. You're in charge of more people than just yourself. When your children grow up and have children of their own, you become a corporal — you have influence with an even larger group. If you live long enough, you may even get to be the general of a vast family tree."

Jared just stared at Wagner.

"My point is simply that every organization has certain levels that you try to rise up to. And levels work." Wagner began to walk again. "Two truths of human nature make them work: First, people like to play or work with others who are at the same skill level. That keeps them from getting either bored or frustrated. And second, people like to advance to the next level. That's what keeps them motivated."

Jared hurried to keep up. "So why choose the army structure over any other?"

"What makes organizations different from each other is not their structure but how rigid or loose the

interactions are between the levels. For instance, in a business climate you might move up or down the ladder for reasons of politics — who you know, what you look like. The army is distinctive because promotion is based on merit."

"And you like that emphasis?" Jared asked.

"In a word, yes," Wagner said. "At Cornerstone, we believe that God has blessed each person He has called to His church with gifts and abilities — as well as opportunities to grow in the knowledge and use of them. In our church, leadership is not based on what people you know, what meetings you attend, how long you have been a member of the church or have been a Christian, or how much you know. It is based on your faithfulness at each level and the fruit God deems to produce."

Jared mulled over his colleague's words. "I think I'm starting to catch on to the idea of levels — just barely." He smiled. "But don't you run into problems with people who, well, like it the way it was?"

"How do you mean?"

"Like someone who wanted to skip a rank," Jared said. "Say a person was talented enough to lead a great Bible study but didn't want to do family devotions."

Wagner sighed and looked at his feet. "We've had people leave for just that reason, especially at the beginning. Sometimes it's hard for people to set down the prestige of leadership to return to the basics. It was a hard decision, but if we had bent the rules for some people, it would have demoralized everyone else. Why work hard when the job will go to someone else who has a friend in high places — you know what I mean?"

He looked at Jared again. "I find this all too often in churches: No one has any idea how to move up in leadership successfully, so they have no motivation to do so. Instead, the church ends up hiring people from the outside — whereas, in the army, all promotion is done from inside the ranks."

Jared laughed. "You're saying you've never brought in outside staff?"

Wagner thought for a moment. "We've never transplanted anyone into a leadership position, no — not without starting as a private."

"I just don't see how that's possible," Jared said. "How did you get pastors for your daughter churches?"

"You're not thinking like an army man yet," Wagner chided. "Most churches who want to daughter a church gather a core leadership team who then go out and try to attract an audience. We send out the audience and let them develop the right leadership. A group of families who are already meeting and worshipping together as a branch of our army is a perfectly viable daughter church under the leadership of a corporal. They simply split off, and then add captains and generals as their growth demands that level of coordination."

"So the pastors come from within the church?" Jared said, as if trying to convince himself. "You don't hire pastors coming out of seminary?"

"I'm proud to say that almost half of the pastors of our daughter churches went to seminary *after* they had birthed the new church," Wagner said. "We have an arrangement with a seminary that allows pastors to complete their course lessons online, and that makes it possible for them to study and minister at the same time. As for the other half — we have taken on seminarians and established church pastors who have a goal of leading a daughter church, but we don't hire them. They have to work through the ranks like anyone else."

"But why go through that hassle?"

Wagner shrugged. "The fact is, most pastors have not learned to preach in the trenches. They went to school and got awarded the generalship, and now they try to act out their notion of what a good general ought to be. It's often forced."

Jared looked away. He felt pierced. He could see himself through his congregation members' eyes; they looked for a model for how they might live, and he was simply guessing at what to show them.

The pair walked along for several minutes without talking. To anyone who saw them they might have looked like the oldest of friends, needing no words to fill the space between them.

"Where do I go from here?" Jared asked in a whisper and was surprised that Wagner heard him.

"I tell everyone who comes to visit me the same thing," Wagner said. "Whether you're starting a new church plant or trying a new approach in an established church, begin by simply humbling yourself and becoming a private in your own life. Become a sergeant in your family. Practice in the trenches, then move up the line, and you'll be surprised how well your sermons and your leadership skills improve."

Up ahead, Jared saw the Cornerstone building come into view. Apparently, they had taken a lap around the block and were coming back to where they had started.

Wagner continued. "Even if the only thing you manage to do is convince your congregation that you're all playing the same game — that your preaching and their daily devotions are essentially the same three tasks of talking, listening, and sharing — then that itself will invigorate your preaching ministry. If you end up taking it beyond that, adding rankings and reading trees, then that will be up to the opportunities God grants and the talent He's given you, won't it?"

Over Wagner's shoulder, Jared watched the group of children playing in the grass, still caught up in a game of baseball. No parents were pushing them to play, no coaches promising pizza after a win. They were there, scampering around, simply for the love of the game. He wanted that feeling again, and he wanted to instill it in the hearts of weary Christians. In that moment, as he nodded absently to Wagner's lingering question, he felt the restlessness in his heart completely melt away.

6

200 MILES

"HON', YOU'RE SO QUIET. IS THERE ANYTHING WRONG?"

Trisha searched her husband's face for an answer, but he was staring blankly at the highway as they zipped past motorists on the long trek home.

"I'm just thinking," he finally said. "Read me more of those notes from the lecture I missed."

He had, in fact, missed several, but she knew the notes he meant — a series on preaching tips. She searched through the pages of her notepad.

"The first tip is: 'Be human,'" she said. "'Let your people see why you still need a Savior. Why should they open up to each other if you don't?' Also, he said: 'Share your own struggle with Scripture. Show them how sometimes you can read a whole passage and not get much, but getting anything makes today's reading a good one.'"

She glanced at Jared to see if he was really listening, but she couldn't tell. "The second tip is: 'Be yourself. If you are not a joke-teller, don't force jokes. If you are an informal guy, be informal. If a storyteller, tell stories. If you are an intellectual analyzer, don't be afraid to use your gift. Be who you are. If you are working too hard at preaching, you are probably trying to be something you are not.'"

Trisha squinted at the notepad. "I can't quite read the third tip — but I'd lay odds it's 'Be' something." Not even a chuckle from Jared. "At any rate, it says here: 'Tap into people's memories. The power of an illustration is not in how dramatic it is, but the degree to which people see their own stories in it. Memories have a way of piling up on each other. That is where the emotion is. When you tell a funny story that happened at the last church picnic, the people laugh — but they are laughing at the combined funny stories of all the church picnics they've attended.'

"And the fourth point is 'Be surly,'" she continued, pretending to read from the paper.

At last, she got a good laugh.

"I'm sorry, Trish," he said, and gave her hand a squeeze. "I've been wrapped up in my thoughts this whole weekend — well, the last several months actually. I've been preoccupied with my questions about preaching, and you and the kids have had to bear the brunt of that." He stole a glance from the road to give her an apologetic smile.

"I thought that if I could just find the answers to my questions, then I could get back to normal and pay attention to you again. But what I think I learned yesterday is that paying attention to you might have been the answer to my question all along."

Trish ruffled Jared's hair and leaned in toward him. "That's really sweet, honey. I have no idea what it means, but it's sweet."

He gave her a broad grin. "What I mean is that I've been so caught up in the spiritual health of the church that

I haven't given proper attention to the spiritual health of our home. You and I haven't had devotions together since ... since when?"

"It's been a long time," she answered softly.

"That needs to change. I'm not saying that we don't do all right fending for ourselves in our spiritual walks, but we could be so much stronger if we talked to God and listened to God together, and together as a family, too. If I'm going to lead a whole congregation to walk with God, I feel I need to start with the Palmquists."

Trisha wasn't sure what to say. "Are you sure?" she asked. "I've always loved when you turn your spiritual attention my way, but I've come to understand that I need to share that part of you with the church."

"I'm positive," he reassured her. "I've been treating the home as a distraction from other ministry, when in fact marriages and families are the basic building blocks of the church. I want to teach others to connect to God in their homes, and that's impossible if I'm not going to do that myself. It's time for me to lead by example."

Trisha gave him a kiss on the cheek and then settled back into her seat.

They sat in silence for a while, watching the stretch of road disappear under their tires. After a while, they passed a sign that announced their city as 200 miles away, and Jared smiled. Their car had a clear destination, but the passengers did not. He had no idea if they would start over at a new church, if they would stay, or if they might even plant a church. All he knew was that — wherever it was God was taking them — it was going to be a great adventure.

"Always be prepared to give an answer to everyone who asks you to give the reason for the hope that you have."

— 1 Peter 3:15

POSTSCRIPT

ALTHOUGH THE TITLE OF THIS BOOK WOULD SEEM TO target a readership of preachers, I trust that it will find its way into the hands of many others. This is a book for all Christians. It assumes that every Christian is called to be a preacher: someone who reads the Word of God with a prayerful attitude and then tells someone else about it. The only difference between pastors and others is how many people you tell.

If you are just an average person in an average church, you might feel powerless to start a revolution in preaching. But you are at least a private in the Lord's army. Develop a strategy of reading daily the manual for Christian living — the Bible. Start with a two-week strategy of reading a verse or a chapter a day. See how it goes. Then tell someone what you are learning. (If you need the support of others, go to www.WheresPhilip.com and ask about the study designed to help you get a personal walk with God.)

If you're married, involve your spouse. Carve out a time just for the two of you to share what God has been saying to you through His Word and prayer. Try it every day for two weeks, and see how you change as you "play the game" of preaching with each other. (If you need the support of others, go to www.WheresPhilip.com and ask about the study designed to help you get a marriage walk with God.)

If you are single, find a friend (or group of friends) to bounce ideas off, sharing what you are discovering about God and the world He has given you. Agree to read the same Bible-reading track. You will naturally talk about what you are reading — the things that inspire you and things that confuse you. Use each other's experiences to grow. Informal Bible studies will happen wherever you and your friends go.

If you have a family, establish family devotions and/or family worship once a week. Memorize verses together. Make your family scheduling time your family praying time. Keep track of prayers answered and prayers yet unanswered. Let the Word and prayer be the things that bring your family together. (Helpful planners and Bible studies designed to get your family into a devotional life can be found at www.WheresPhilip.com.)

Remember, every aspect of the church service you mimic in your personal life or your family life can make Sunday worship more meaningful. The more you're seeking God in your Bible reading and telling others, the more you'll connect with the pastor's efforts to do the same. The better you learn how to sing or play an instrument, the more resonance you'll find in the hymns and choruses. The more you make hospitality and generosity part of your daily walk with God, the more you will understand the church's role to reach out to the world in love.

If you find that your personal and family devotions are going well, involve others — friends and other families. The excitement of new people will help keep you going. Who knows where God may take you from there? Perhaps, after you've made a consistent habit of your gatherings, you will offer to share your experiences in front of the church. Maybe people will see the difference the Word and prayer are making in your life and will want to join in. Perhaps each family in your group will start a new group with new people who want to be playing the "preaching game," and your church might never be the same again.

To my fellow pastors: I hope this book has not disappointed you. Most books on preaching are filled with tips and examples that you can immediately apply with a certain measure of success. This book did not do that. (Although there are a few good tips listed in the last chapter — I didn't want to totally let you down.)

The truth is, most of us preachers are not going to improve much in our delivery no matter how many tips we get. No matter how hard you work on your preaching skills, only ten percent of you will ever make it into the top ten percent of pulpiteers. Most of you (all right, most of *us*) will never be anything more than average.

You may never be a great preacher, but your preaching can be great — great in effect. The secret is to create a culture of preaching in your church, an environment where everyone is spurring on one another in the process of walking with God and sharing those experiences. Then your sermon becomes the culmination of the congregation's spiritual focus each week. Simply put, the power of preaching is not in the pastor on the podium; it is in the people and their practices.

What would happen if the sermon came from the same Bible passages the people were reading that week?

Anticipation: All week long the people would be wondering what the chosen message of the week would be.

Nostalgia: The sermon would trigger the emotion of recognition and connect people to something familiar.

Accountability: The knowledge that everyone else in the church will be keeping up with the reading, and that the sermon will assume a familiarity with the text, will give incentive to complete the homework.

Community: After a week of conversations and prayers revolving around the same Scriptures, the sermon will gather people physically just as they have been gathered mentally and spiritually. These shared experiences will create a deep bond.

Participation: In a way, all the people in the church will prepare the message every week, interacting with the text and having their hearts changed. You can use individuals or groups of people in the preparation and perhaps even in the delivery of the message.

Changing the practices of your congregation will not be easy. It will not happen overnight. It will not happen just because you tell people to change. It will happen, by the grace of God, when you model the process first in your own life — when you share it with others and inspire them with your personal commitment and influence in their lives.

That is the challenge put forth to you in this book. I hope that my use of an army metaphor, or my tip of the hat to John Wesley, does not distract you from that core principle. If the army jargon is a stumbling block for you, feel free to substitute the motif with something that works better for you or your community. (My wife was lobbying for a quilting metaphor.) As for me, I chose it because an army general seemed the clearest example of a leader who had worked through the ranks — one who drew people's attention and respect from having once been in their shoes. I also liked it because all soldiers are playing the same game, and all seek to advance as far as their gifts, abilities, and opportunities present themselves.

As for my interest in Wesley — I must admit that, since I come from the Calvinist tradition, he is an odd choice for me to use as a role model. Our two camps have a long history of dispute over the emphasis on God's sovereignty vs. man's responsibility in the Christian journey. This book includes some of each: I have set forth tasks for us to *do* to grow closer to God, which might make some readers from my tradition squirm, but I have tried to emphasize equally that God is the one who determines what efforts will bear fruit, not us. In the end, it is important to remember that growing closer to God is never the result of just one thing — our habits with God, our knowledge of God, our commitment to God, or our experience of God — but all of them together, which are the basis of a *relationship* with God that transcends any "silver bullet" approach. The habits outlined in this book should be viewed as just the first steps on the path toward deeper intimacy with God.

This book is not a simple blueprint or a formula for preaching success; rather, it is a swarm of ideas that serve as a jumping-off point for your own quest for a renewed preaching ministry Use it creatively. And may God bless you on your journey.

If you would like help creating a culture of preaching in your church or denomination, contact selzinga@bibleleague.org for information on seminars or consultations.

THE FINAL WORD

This book was not written just to get you excited about sermons, or what preaching could do in your church and your life. It was written to introduce you to a new paradigm, a new way of thinking about your relationship with God, your family, and your mission in life.

This new way of thinking starts with the small before the big, gets you to see the church from the bottom up not the top down, advocates using the average many before the talented few, believes in walking with God before talking about Him. This paradigm says, "Let's create playing fields where all people get a chance to play and develop at their own level." This paradigm asks: "Who knows what God has planned for you? Who knows what God can do through you?"

This book applies this way of thinking to preaching. If you want to see how this thinking plays out in other areas, check out the rest of this series:

The Secret to a Great Music Ministry

The Secret to a Great Discipleship Ministry

The Secret to a Great Evangelism Ministry

The Secret to a Great Leadership Ministry

WORKS CITED

p. 4: *"Every accent, every emphasis ... "*
   Benjamin Franklin, *Memoirs of the Life and Writing of Benjamin Franklin*, Vol. I, p. 87.

p. 4: *"I went up on a mount ... "*
   George Whitefield, *Journals* (London: Banner of Truth Trust, 1960), p. 216.

p. 5: *"Having no righteousness ... "*
   John Gillies, ed., *Memoirs of the Reverend George Whitefield* (New Haven: Whitmore and Buckingham and H. Mansfield, 1834), p. 28.

p. 8: *"If that be the case ... "*
   John A. Newton, *Susanna Wesley and the Puritan Tradition in Methodism* (London: Epworth Press, 1968), pp. 87-88.

p. 9: *"a little gathered Church ... "*
   Ibid., p. 53.

p. 11: *"It took no training ... "*
   D. Michael Henderson, *John Wesley's Class Meeting* (Nappanee, IN: Evangel Publishing House, 1997), p. 101.

ORDERING INFORMATION

The ideas in this book are meant to be shared with other people. Accordingly, we've made this book as inexpensive as possible so that you can afford to buy one for anyone in leadership (pastor, deacon, small group leader, ministry coordinator, Sunday School teacher) and for those who could step up in leadership (everyone else in your church). You may purchase this book in lots of 10 for $2.99 (USD) apiece. Individual copies are only $3.99.

To buy online, visit our web page for international ordering at **http://www.wheresphilip.com/preaching**.

To order by mail or phone, use the following contact information for your country:

UNITED STATES:	AUSTRALIA:
1-800-871-5445	1-800-800-937
Bible League	The Bible League
PO Box 28000	PO Box 4071
Chicago, IL 60628	Werrington NSW 2747
CANADA:	NEW ZEALAND:
1-800-363-9673	+9-846-5111
The Bible League	Bible League
PO Box 5037	PO Box 77-047
Burlington ON, L7R 3Y8	Mt Albert, Auckland 1030